D1559194

The Opposite of ObamaCare

How a free enterprise philosophy would

dramatically reduce health care prices

Joseph A. Gilbertson

Punching Bag Media, LLC

1515 N. Federal Highway

Boca Raton, Florida 33432

Acknowledgements

I would like to thank the staff at Punching Bag Media, especially Sean Gibbons and Alice Green for their contributions, both in discussions of the topic and in editing. They truly helped turn this "sow's ear" into a "silk purse" insofar as the content warrants.

We would also like to acknowledge our fellow conservative publishers who have contributed through their writings, their passion and their hard work on this subject matter.

Table of Contents

Introduction

I wrote this book because I'm watching ObamaCare unfold as an unmitigated disaster; health care costs are sky rocketing and my own health care costs are rising by more than 20% per year, even though I'm perfectly healthy and in decent shape.

The Opposite of ObamaCare is about returning our health care system to a free enterprise perspective, where individual choice rules. It's about dismantling ObamaCare (actually two separate pieces of legislation — the Patient Protection and Affordable Care Act and the Health Care and Education Reconciliation Act) - a massive government/insurance infrastructure tending to socialism - to create a vibrant competitive environment.

If structured correctly, competition will send pricing spiraling down, all the while maintaining high quality and widely available health care. This is about turning the most powerful capitalist engine in the world toward making health care affordable to everyone, not because the government says so, but because free enterprise, technology and innovation have found ways to make health care efficient, pervasive and convenient.

At this rate, ObamaCare will accomplish exactly the opposite of what we were promised. Every action purported to lower prices has caused a rise. We are separating the patient from the doctor with layers of bureaucracy. The result is not affordable health care, but a two-tiered health care system, a very expensive and effective one for the elites and a substandard system for the middle and lower class people, who won't be able to afford better.

The health industry has already been damaged, doctors are leaving their practices, customers are paying dramatically higher rates for their insurance, etc. Perhaps this sounds gratuitous and politically partisan, but I intend to illustrate.

If this keeps up, future health care will no longer be in the hands of the individual, it will just be too expensive for any ordinary individual to keep up with. Perhaps it will be our employer, perhaps it will be the government, but the consequences of this will be devastating as quality starts to decrease, as it must. The rich will be fine, because a vibrant black market will rise up (as it did in the Soviet Union, as you will see later). The middle class and poor will be stuck with substandard care.

I'm not saying this *might* happen. I'm saying it *will* happen.

If we don't restructure away from ObamaCare and put the system right, *IT CAN'T HAPPEN ANY OTHER WAY!*

This book is much more about free enterprise and economics than about medicine. ObamaCare shows a lack of understanding of these principles; it is a perfect example of what not to do.

Who am I?

Am I a health care expert? No.

I'm a farm boy from Kentucky, earned advanced degrees from reputable universities in engineering and business, I've run a couple of companies, done some Intelligence Community service and I've studied this mess for a long time. My expertise is marketing, media influence, propaganda, mass psychology, and certain kinds of political theory. I have some exposure to the business of medicine in a consulting capacity, but I have no credentials in the medical field, nor do I need them. This work is entirely based on the principles of free enterprise, which I have been practicing most of my life.

I'm writing this in frustration because I don't see where anyone else has put together a comprehensive opposition plan taking these factors into account. The smart people in Congress and in nationally known think tanks should have presented a free enterprise plan to replace ObamaCare by now, but it appears I have to step up.

I'm sure some of the great intellectual beings out will criticize this work. I've been accused before of "writing poorly" by academic elites, who corrected my grammar but couldn't seem to grasp the concepts. I will freely accept constructive criticisms and may even write an update with better data and better ideas. Because I've risked my life for America (almost a 'deader' on four separate occasions…), it's my right and my duty to speak up. This is my best shot at providing some sorely need guidance to America's leadership.

Theory - Basic Principles

To understand my arguments you must understand a few basic theories of free enterprise. These are not difficult and in fact are completely intuitive, but you have to *believe* them for the logic to stick with you. So if you don't quite follow some of the later material re-read this section. The principles are:

A. Whatever you subsidize you get more of.

B. Businesses are smarter than government.

C. Socialism is never productive.

D. Prices go down when competition is present, based on price and quality.

A. *Whatever You Subsidize You Get More Of.*

This is called the Law of Subsidies, **whatever you subsidize you get more of, and whatever you tax you get less of.** It seems obvious, if you subsidize green t-shirts by paying kids $20 to wear them, you get a lot of kids wearing green t-shirts. If you pay farmers extra to grow radishes, you will have a flood of radishes on the market. But what you have to realize is this principle is not just a passing thought or a minor annoyance. The principle that 'whatever you subsidize you get more of' is *an overwhelming economic and social driver that applies on a global basis.*

For example, if we are talking about welfare in the U.S., the more benefits you provide in the welfare system, the more welfare recipients you get. And oh, by the way, if you subsidize starving folks in the desert by feeding them without helping them become self-sufficient; all you get is more starving folks in the desert (they have kids, plus they attract people from across the border who also want to be fed, giving up whatever productive activity helping them survive before).

How does this apply to health care? If you start subsidizing people's health care you get more people who need help because it's easier to accept help than to help yourself. And incidentally, if you subsidize the medical bills for these folks, you get higher prices.

The opposite is true as well, whatever you tax you get less of. This has been used for good in many ways. For example, the government taxes cigarettes and liquor, so prices go up and people buy lower quantities. But if you tax business you take resources away from business for expansion - you get less business. If you reduce taxes on business, you effectively subsidize it, so you get more business. Anyone who has run a business can find better uses for the money paid in taxes.

People occasionally subsidize good things. For example, the government subsidizes certain farm products to keep farms from disappearing; otherwise we would at the mercy of other countries for our food. The government often subsidizes military defense of its allied nations to make sure they can defend themselves and don't get swallowed up by aggressive neighbors (therefore you get more or bigger allies). My brother, a former representative to the New Hampshire house passed the "net metering" law in New Hampshire to make it more cost effective to install solar panels, an inexpensive and well leveraged subsidy of alternative energy (actually a breakdown of a barrier to entry...).

Case Study – The Community Reinvestment Act

Unfortunately, often what you think you are subsidizing is NOT what you are getting more of.

The Community Reinvestment Act of 1977 (CRA) was a well-intentioned act designed to provide resources to break down barriers in racially divided communities. The idea was to subsidize loans to folks who wanted to own their own homes in depressed areas, normally poor investments for banks. What we were supposed to "get more of" were home owners in depressed areas who would better take care of their houses, and who would care about the state of their community.

However this act was reinterpreted and enhanced in 1991, 1994, 1995, 1999, and 2005, evolving radically into something else. Since these loans were effectively backed by the government, it became an all-encompassing subsidy of high risk, unstable loans.

So for a short time we had more home owners, but most under this program could barely afford them. Lenders realized this and started to trade and concentrate these high risk loans (lenders were effectively subsidized, so you got more of those too!). The tipping point was tiny shift in interest rates making payments higher. The result? Massive foreclosures and over 800,000 homes lost just in 2008. This was an incredible lack of foresight and lack of understanding of free enterprise by our government in passing these laws.

The CRA was a "socialist" method of solving a problem, shoved forward with the capitalist engine of the most powerful financial system on Earth. The government thought it was subsidizing the American Dream, it was really subsidizing foolish risk.

There are hundreds of similar cases. Countless well-meaning charities have created more suffering than they heal, creating options that entrap people rather than allowing a natural course of tough decision-making that might actually lead to progress and improvement.

I'm not saying subsidies are good or bad. I'm saying politicians often don't realize that a) they are not encouraging what they think they are and b) if you put a powerful free enterprise engine behind almost anything, you may get way more of something you never bargained for. One purpose of this book is to make sure our leaders analyze EVERY law for socialist characteristics, unintended consequences and the rule of subsidies.

Just to bring this around to point, ObamaCare includes massive subsidies that extend into the middle class. Once you have millions of people addicted to an unsustainable health care system, a massive meltdown will occur.

B. Businesses are Smarter than Government.

I'm not saying that government doesn't have smart people. I spent 12 years in government, and some of the people I worked with were stone cold geniuses. But for any given industry, business people vastly outnumber the experts and analysts in Washington, D.C. Private industry is better motivated, better focused and it pays better for top talent.

Consider in Washington D.C. how people think. They want to be powerful or be next to powerful people. A Congressman wants to be re-elected, wants people to like him. A lobbyist wants to represent his clients to powerful politicians. A think tanker wants funding from politicians or lobbyists. You have a whole mix of competing and opposing agendas.

Views in Washington, D.C. are not chosen for their efficiency and effectiveness in increasing commercial productivity, they are chosen for efficiency and effectiveness in getting the politician re-elected. I'm not saying this is a bad way to do political business, but while the pursuit of their personal goals often results in some nifty compromises, it is not the competitive skill used in unbridled capitalism.

By comparison, businesses are much more focused and narrowly motivated. You have an owner who is very interested and enjoys his business, be it plumbing, doctoring, farming, manufacturing or whatever. Beyond that it's about profit. All other things being equal, it's better to be a rich plumber than a poor one, better to be a rich farmer than a poor one, etc.

This is life and death for the business, they have only two modes, growing and dying. If you think you are standing still, you are not. You are dying. It's a powerful motivator to find new ways to profit.

(Think of any business as a plant. Did you ever have a plant that stopped growing? Yeah, it's dead...)

So a businessman who is actually in the throes of business is motivated to know his business better than anyone in Washington possibly could. And these guys communicate, boy do they ever. Let me give an example.

I had an uncle who owned an auto body shop, a very successful one. He also happened to be president of the local garage owners association, which met once a month. Each month at their meetings 30 or 40 garage owners would talk about new techniques, new ways of doing business, avoiding pitfalls, technologies and a lot more (apparently much drinking involved...), much of it coming down from the national organization. If someone found a simple solution for a difficult problem in Memphis, it eventually got to my uncle's group in Louisville. As a result, my uncle and his fellow members operated the most modern shops with the latest techniques and were some of the busiest and up-to-date body shops in the city.

Could anyone in Washington know the body shop business in Louisville, Kentucky better than these gentlemen? Not possible.

I'm a science fiction buff so let's talk about the principle of the "hive mind." Sounds mysterious and disgusting right? But the principle is whenever you have a group of people in cooperation, the whole of the group has more experience than any individual could have and can generate more information to be consumed by group. The faster the communications in one of these groups, the more the ideas develop and the faster the growth of the group intelligence. The internet and the advent of social networks have put this on steroids. In other words, the "hive mind" for plumbers, body shop owners or other groups gets smarter and smarter until every member has or can get the latest and best ideas and practices. These groups, in hive mind fashion, are largely self-organizing and very powerful. The result of the association is the individual operations become more efficient and higher in quality.

Now I'm sure my uncle never thought of his group as a "hive" but I guarantee no group in D.C. consumes knowledge as voraciously as private industry does.

In the case of the mortgage meltdown described above, banks were moving at breakneck speed to accumulate wealth; the government could not keep up with what was happening. Each company was dissecting the laws to maximize profit and reduce risk for themselves. It was self-organizing. When someone made money, everyone else found out how, joined in, and leapfrogged to the next level. The government and think tank watchdogs had no real grasp of how fast these institutions were moving just out of simple self-interest, until it was too late!

Case Study – Holes in the Financial System

The financial industry is complex, stocks, bonds, loan packages, commodities, extending to derivatives of derivatives of derivatives. Derivative investments exist so complex, only a handful of people even understand how they function. Certain buildings on Long Island are full of Ph.D. physicists who do nothing but try to figure out ways to game the financial system while staying within the law. Often they succeed, and D.C.'s efforts to find and close these loop holes may take years or may never happen at all. D.C. is simply outclassed by the private financial community.

As an example of how this has worked in a bad way, Michael Lewis, author of the book Flash Boys (1), talks about how high frequency traders (his example company is Spread Networks) had developed a system to take advantage of a sub-millisecond difference in communications speeds between exchange markets. Because they had arranged for more direct communications routes, they could monitor orders in multiple exchanges and as blocks of shares were traded they could actually insert their buy orders in the midst of someone else's order and sell those shares to the order party at a higher price.

There was no law covering this, no think tank experts on top of it and no way for the government to catch on. It was merely a hole in the system where they could take advantage. This hole was worth literally billions of dollars.

A young Brad Katsuyama who was running the Royal Bank of Canada's stock desk helped to fix the problem by inserting a delay in the faster lines to remove the advantage. This was not a government or regulatory solution, but his own initiative in protecting his employer and righting a wrong in the system. But it illustrates how fast-moving a knowledgeable, creative and self-interested private industry can be compared to the government and regulatory agencies looking after them. Again, to summarize – business is smarter than government.

With both the stock exchange trading system and the sub-prime mortgage industry, the workings were so complex and private organizations moved so fast, the smartest regulatory minds could not conceive of the consequences until it was too late

ObamaCare is more complex and has a hundred times as many players - can we afford to wait for private industry to game it?

This is the principle that business is smarter than government. I'm not saying government is stupid, I'm saying the collective brains of private industry will always out-think the individual brains within the government. The solution is obvious - make sure the laws align the interests of private industry with the interests of America.

C. Socialist Strategies are Never Productive.

Let's talk about what socialism is, why it never actually produces positive value, and why it is in fact a "negative feedback system" in our parlance. The principle of socialism is that all productive capacities are *owned* by the government and the products generated are *distributed* by the government. Karl Marx describes it succinctly (actually first spoken by Louis Blanc, 1851) "**From each according to his abilities, to each according to his needs.**"

It's easy enough to prove. Just use the Law of Subsidies, in a conceptual way, applied to that statement. **If you tax "abilities" you will get fewer people of ability. If you subsidize "needs" you will get more needy people.** In a true "negative feedback" fashion, it consumes its own productivity until it fails. That's why the Soviet Union needed to continually expand. It had to. But there is more.

Human beings are at their core instinctual, these instincts being the means by which man has survived since his ancestors arose from the primordial ooze. Evolutionary psychology is the study of these instincts, ranging from scratching an itch (ever had an itch you couldn't scratch, the instinct to scratch makes you suffer until you get it) to fear and avoidance of death (a strong death avoidance instinct comes in very handy when you are in a primeval jungle with saber-toothed cats). Most instinctual needs are easily taken care of in modern America, food and shelter are readily obtained, and death avoidance is not so much a daily thing as it had been in mankind's past.

Two instincts related to reproduction dominate most of our lives nowadays. One is the parenting, we love our children. The instinct to protect them and give them advantages is exceedingly strong. The second is even more pervasive in society and has been described as "competition for mates and resources" i.e. the process of finding and winning the woman (or man) with whom we want to bear children. So yes, competition is an instinct; it has helped the human race succeed, reproduce and improve through thousands of generations.

I would estimate in America satisfying these two instincts covers 80-90 percent of the activities in our daily lives, depending on where you are in life. If you do not yet have children then competition for mates and resources is likely a good deal of your focus. If you have a mate and children then your competition for resources may transfer in part to competition for the success of your children. This instinct is there, you want your children to survive, thrive and be happy. If your ancestors had not cared for their children then from an evolutionary standpoint your family line would have been long ago extinct. Parents often forego their own advancement to live vicariously through their children. So the children learn to compete (actually learn how to do this best from their parents) and the human race continues.

And this is the problem, socialism short circuits competition.

Socialism is designed to rid society of individual competition, which is one of the strivings that makes us human. The major socialist experiment of the twentieth century, the Soviet Union, failed miserably but not after leader after leader tried to fit humankind into a socialist mold. Lenin and Stalin decided that the way to affect socialism and pave the road to communism was to get rid of the misfits who would not accept the socialist construct. Lenin went on to kill 6 million "misfits" in his population. Stalin killed over

30 million of his own people over the following 30 years or so. (These were actually attempts at "eugenics," i.e. the breeding of a new kind of human being). It still didn't work.

When the Soviet Union finally fell in 1991, the black market (a highly competitive free enterprise system both at its best and worst) was so strong and pervasive that it became the backbone of the new Russian economy and of the breakaway Soviet territories and countries. This illustrates how strong competition is ingrained in human nature; free enterprise in the form of a thriving black market emerges even under the threat of death.

But let's illustrate through example. Suppose you are part of small community with limited resources in the socialist world. You have children and one of them decides she wants to play the piano. Unfortunately the government has only allotted one piano teacher to your area, and the last slot with the only teacher available has been taken by the son of the mayor. So your child is on a permanent waiting list. Someone has decided (remember "each according to his abilities to each according to his needs") and clearly the mayor's child has greater needs than yours!!!

Being a good and competitive parent you want the best for your child, in fact you are invested in your child's success. You want your child to be happy and prominent and to live a better life than yours and you believe learning the piano will help your child. Note that your desire is not anything selfish. Your desire is a manifestation of the competitive and parenting compulsions, entirely unselfish and based in deep seated instinctual drives.

So what are you going to do about it? Will you accept the state's word and give up on giving your child this advantage? Or would you find a free enterprise style, perhaps work extra for a neighbor to get extra resources to be used to bribe the piano teacher to teach your child in his off hours? While this may not be allowed in a socialist system (and indeed is a forbidden corruption of its "fair" distribution system!) it is a classic example of free enterprise. Everyone wins, but the socialist state experiences a bit of naughty corruption.

In this case, socialism does not serve you well because you wouldn't take for granted the state's assertion that your child shouldn't learn to play the piano. The competitive instinct means you believe you can win. The socialist distribution of goods did not take your faith and love for your child into account, but free enterprise solved the problem and produced more piano playing students.

At the same time, the work you did for your neighbor to pay for the piano lessons also provided benefit for your neighbor, for you, for the piano teacher and for your child. I would term this a "positive feedback system."

Now think in terms of something more important than piano lessons. Perhaps your child is sick with a deadly disease and the socialist system has decided to spend set amount of it rigid budget in the cure, and others will get the cure before your child does. Do you care that other children may be saved by your child's sacrifice? Intellectually perhaps you can understand, since by that time in your socialist existence you should be thoroughly indoctrinated. The state has already decided your child has a lower priority compared to others. But any parent will move heaven and earth and even risk their own life to save their child.

In a free enterprise system, the parent who is willing to pay the most wins. However if a cure is needed and people are willing to pay, the free enterprise system makes more available. In fact that market may be smart enough to build an infrastructure to make sure those needs are taken care of, and anticipate when they are needed and invest precious resources in making a stockpile. Not because theoretically this is good for humankind, but because it's a profitable venture and the markets support it (i.e. satisfies my own personal needs for mates and resources). Again, self-interest motivates higher productivity - not sympathy, not civic duty.

Also think in terms of imagination and creativity in creating new medical solutions. Do you believe it's better to have a few government experts determining which research is necessary and promising, and reviewing it once a year? Or is it better to have 10's of thousands of self-interested researchers looking to help the world but also to make a profit? Remember these guys love doing research, it's their life's work, but it's better to be a rich researcher than a poor one.

I talk about free enterprise as a "positive feedback" system meaning the needs of each self-interested entity reinforce free enterprise, and productivity spirals upwards. Socialism is a "negative feedback" system, because the feedback discourages individual production and encourages its own corruption.

The socialist government determines your benefits based on what it thinks are your needs. Extra productivity by individuals not only provides no commensurate benefit, but is discouraged as corruption of the socialist principles. Productivity in every large scale socialist endeavor has been shown to have spiraled downward.

One might have a look at the socialist style health care systems around the world and declare them successful. But if you look at the underpinnings, you will find they are not self-sufficient. They actually require a great deal of government support to maintain. In fact, the "single payer" strategy is specifically designed to obscure the total cost of such a system, since taxpayer dollars are mixed with patient payments.

Bottom line – because it discourages productivity, a socialist strategy always requires more resources to support it than it produces. Without self-interest and competition, workers are not motivated to put in the extra work, buck the system to make improvements or think about new ways to things better. Competition is hard, free enterprise is hard. If your instinctual desires are satisfied (or indeed short circuited by a socialist system), you have no reason to go the extra mile. Capitalists call the results of the extra mile "profit."

Of course, as sometimes happens, socialist governments may find short term gains in productivity by making sweeping changes on a mass scale. But these gains pale in comparison to what happens when thousands of business owners are empowered with knowledge, capital and free will (remember businesses are smarter than government…).

The Soviet Union had traction for a while, but it was borrowed traction. As they absorbed more countries into satellite status they were able to keep up with the "negative feedback loop" of socialism by gutting the resources of those nations. It couldn't last.

D. *Prices Go Down with Competition Based on Price and Quality*

This is very intuitive:

a) If you have two options perceived to be the same quality, you choose the lower priced option.

b) If you have two options at the same price, you choose the perceived higher quality.

Obviously "quality" in a medical practice is an individual perception. Quality might best be based on the percentage of good outcomes, if you happen to have access to that information. Quality in some people's minds may be determined by convenience (i.e. near your house), office amenities, the attractiveness of the nurses, or the fact that the doctor is your cousin and likes you better.

Note a new principle here. The Law of Supply vs. Demand, taught in every business school, is actually quite wrong in application. It should read "The Law of Perceived Supply vs. Perceived Demand." Any good marketer will tell you he can create a sense of demand ("everybody is buying this") and scarcity of supply ("get this while supplies last!"), to get a higher price from consumers even when the consumer's perceptions are at odds with reality.

So we are not necessarily talking about *actual* quality which may be impossible to determine when the buying decision is made. We are talking about *perceived* quality. Perceived quality can be affected by good marketing, a good sales pitch, or recommendations from your friends. "Risk" is a factor in the quality decision, if your friends like a particular medical facility then you may believe it is less risky for you.

Price can also be a "perceived" value. Are you paying on a monthly plan? Is there a deep first year discount? Is credit available? Very few American consumers are able to do "net present value" calculations, but most have a good grasp of their own financial situation and how a pricing plan would affect their short term budget.

So you make a decision based on your perception of price and quality, and the vendors of products compete on all of the factors involved in your decision. The "actual" price and quality numbers can be bent somewhat with good marketing strategy; these vendors look for ways to improve your perception of their price and quality to win your business, often adding real value. Production efficiency goes up and value for the customer constantly improves.

Now think about how the insurance companies and your employer work together. You never shopped for this so you had no part in the decisions on price and quality. Your employer did the shopping, but his "price" and "quality" factors are with respect to his business, not your health care. The decisions you make within your own health plan may optimize quality within limits (or may be very good quality at a very high price). You will find the "best" doctor who happens to accept your insurance plan. Whether he is expensive or not is irrelevant.

We're not saying this is a sinister collaboration between your employer and the health insurance company. After all, they are doing their best to meet your needs. But a few dozen insurance companies competing for business customers in the 10's of thousands is nowhere near as powerful as would be 100's of thousands of doctors competing for 10's of millions of patients, as you will see below.

And when you look at combining all of the employees from a company onto a single plan, the result looks an awful lot like "from each according to his abilities, to each according to his needs," doesn't it?

Theory – How Insurance has Socialist Effects

Is insurance a socialist pastime? Certainly not. Insurance executives are hard hitting capitalists. In fact insurance companies are some of the largest and most profitable entities in the world. However the concept of insurance has something important in common with socialism. It makes distribution decisions like a socialist entity might, and puts a massive bureaucracy between the buyer and the seller. You are no longer shopping based on the price and quality of the actual medical care.

First let me say something about the insurance industry. I don't want to paint them as fiends; they are simply capitalists who are providing an absolutely necessary service. The executives I met in my one (extremely short) consulting gig in the health insurance industry were passionate about their support of doctors and in providing good care. They are good people. I will not disparage them here nor do I want to put them out of business.

Insurance reduces risk. This is necessary and entirely allowable in a free enterprise economy. Without the concept and the industry of insurance, our country could not have grown to the greatness it has achieved.

But...

Socialism, in simple terms, is where people provide everything to the government and the government then provides "fairly" back to the people. It seems like such a nice and friendly system because everyone is taken care of. Maybe no one gets rich, but also no one starves, at least as long as part of society is productive enough to provide for all of the people. We've described this before; it has severe drawbacks that must be paid for.

The process of insurance, while admittedly a completely different kind of institution, has some commonality with socialism. A whole lot of people pay into the system, and then an administration distributes benefits according to needs.

But by doing this, they short circuit competition, and isolate patients from the price and quality factors they should be seeking. Patients don't have to worry about price because insurance covers it, so they choose the highest quality product allowed. Since payments to doctors are transparent to the patient, a de facto subsidy occurs and prices go up. When the patient's premium goes up, the patient doesn't associate this with the doctor's pricing to the insurance company. The doctor can (and may have to...) slowly raise his prices without fear of losing customers because the customer doesn't know and doesn't care. It's nobody's fault, but the lack of transparency sends costs spiraling up.

As insurance becomes more and more necessary (i.e. no longer a choice because even non-emergency health care costs too much), insurance provides a socialist environment for their customers. Neither the patient nor the doctor is motivated to be more efficient because their individual efforts would not help in the least. Negative feedback applies and costs spiral higher.

Let's illustrate. Say you have kids and you are picking a doctor for them. Your employer provides your insurance plan. Are you going to take them to the doctor with the linoleum and the plastic plants in the waiting room or the one that has carpet and real plants? They cost the same, your insurance pays for either. Note these irrelevant factors have direct impact on the price of the service but not necessarily any impact on real quality (even great doctors can have poor taste in carpet…). But since you have no ability to determine how good the doctor is when you choose him, e.g., which one is more educated or has a better success rate, you are going to choose your doctor based on his carpet and the real plants.

Competition for practical purposes is based on cosmetics. The real factors are opaque and unavailable to the consumer. The quality and success rate of a medical practice, if describe in medical statistical terminology, may even be too complex to understand.

Solution Part #1 - Limits to Insurance Companies

A. *Insurance vs. Maintenance*

Insurance

Insurance is a spreading out of risk of certain significant, costly and unpleasant events among members, each of whom is unlikely to experience those events. In the medical world, breaking a leg is unlikely, cancer is unlikely, a heart attack is unlikely, any number of strange life threatening diseases are unlikely, and the risk should be insurable.

These events happen rarely, and when they do they can drain the resources of an average individual to the point where his life may crash, the drain on resources interrupting the continuity of a well-planned life. If one could predict the timing and nature of such an event, one could save up and prepare for it. But an unexpected problem at a vulnerable time could turn a successful life into a failure.

Insurance relies on the statistical calculations of large populations to estimate the total risk and how much it will cost. Using sophisticated demographic studies with statistics and past history, insurance companies can accurately predict how many of each catastrophic event will occur (but not to whom they will occur) within their insured population or "risk pool."

For each person to save up enough to handle a major catastrophic event would mean a lot of savings. But say only 1 of 10 of the population actually experiences a major event. That means that to insure a population, each person need only raise and contribute 10% of the required amount for safety and the entire population is taken care of. A guaranteed payment of 10% against a possible loss of 100% can be a great benefit. Granted no one gets their premiums back, but then again if the money has to be in reserve for a catastrophe, you can't use the money anyway.

So it makes sense to contribute a small amount to protect the entire risk pool rather than try to mitigate all risk by yourself. Even if you could cover the cost of a major event, what if there were two?

To administer a program like this, the insurance companies charge a premium of about 40% over the actual cost of the risk. (2) This may seem like a high percentage but it includes all of the billing, the sales people, the benefits administrators and a lot more. The insurance industry works hard to maintain the best possible efficiency and they are pretty good at it.

Maintenance

On the other hand, maintenance costs in our scenario include the cost of checkups, occasional visits to a specialist, medicine we certainly need, like aspirin, flu shots, antibiotics, eye drops, antihistamines and others. If you have children, this would include vaccinations, stitches for minor injuries, normal childhood diseases, etc. If you have allergies, treatments may be chronic. Other maintenance items might be by choice, like birth control, hair loss medicine. In a broader sense, perhaps your gym membership, vitamins and other health related could be considered maintenance items as well.

There are other costs that are expensive but also predictable. These are not really a matter of risk, in fact the timing is easily known. For example pregnancy and the birth of child can be planned very precisely. This can be a major expenditure, but most births go fairly smoothly. Right now your insurance plan pays for all of it (plus 40%!).

Would all of this not be more cost effective if there were a maintenance plan without the 40% up charge from the insurance company, and then a small premium in case there are complications?

If you are diabetic, should your insurance pay for these costs? You may have to have medicine for the rest of your life, if your insurance pays for this, then certainly you are paying for it in your insurance premiums, plus the 40%. Does the insurance company deserve a cut, just for taking your money and giving it to someone else?

Some would say "Hey I'm paying enough for insurance this better be covered!" But the fact is if it were being paid another way, your insurance costs would be less.

Bundling

Bundling is the practice of combining disparate services into "one low price." Cable companies are especially good at this, they will not let you select individual channels, you must pick groupings of channels. It is not a particularly sinister practice, it's just a normal efficient marketing strategy.

However bundling takes away transparency in pricing. If you buy cable bundle you have no idea how much the individual channels cost. You may be subsidizing the Spanish channels or the shopping channels even though you don't speak Spanish and you find the shopping channels tedious.

In health insurance, by bundling insurance and maintenance together into a single plan, you have no idea how much you pay for each, which obscures the basic principle of shopping based on price and quality. While from the point of view of the insurance company this simplifies things and allows them to provide a more comprehensive product at a higher price point, insurance and maintenance as I defined them above are very different products.

B. Separate Insurance and Maintenance

Insurance companies currently bundle office visits and normal maintenance items in with insurance coverage. You now have an all-inclusive plan and won't have to pay for anything except your co-payments. It's convenient and easy and inserts the insurance company into major parts of your life.

But of course it takes choices away from the individual, and removes any visibility into pricing.

Let's examine how this works right now.

Insurance companies love this because they get to tack on their profit margin to more stuff. Their gross margin as I mentioned before is about 40%. So whatever the nominal charge would be from your doctor, 40% more is worked into your insurance premiums. You get nothing free, this is calculated to the penny by insurance actuaries, and the insurance company makes a profit .

These fees are charged by the insurance company but there is no insurance benefit of spreading risk on maintenance items, because there is no risk. It's maintenance, everyone has to pay it.

The office visits and other benefits still have to be paid for, the insurance company is not getting these for free. But by bundling, the insurance company takes their profit on more services. This is not "insurance" it's merely a time payment plan, more expensive than paying it outright or doing a time payment plan on just those services. Prices HAVE to go up, even if they don't go up immediately. I'm not blaming the insurance companies for this, they are responding to market pressures and customer requests.

How to we fix this? Let's make a new law.

Insurance companies should be strictly prohibited from "bundling" maintenance items with insurance.

As described above, "maintenance" items are things that must be paid for as a matter of course, for example checkups, flu shots, birth control, aspirin, cough medicine, etc. as described in the previous section. Everyone has these expenses, why would you want insurance to pay for them (adding their profit margin)? Chronic conditions and predictable expense like having a baby should be put on a time payment plan.

Insurance should be for high risk items, things that are not likely to happen to any individual. Again, these might include a broken leg, cancer, a stroke, a heart attack, etc. The premiums and payments are statistically based; insurance companies have roomfuls of actuaries working to spread the risk accurately.

I might further recommend that insurance be made more honest in its character. Right now when you get insurance you are placed in a "risk pool" in which a certain percentage are statistically expected to have certain medical issues. The problem is if you happen to develop one of the problems they expect someone in their pool to have, they immediately kick you out of that risk pool and raise your pricing. Does this make sense?

If those problems were expected, then haven't you just fulfilled their prediction? Why would you be kicked out of the risk pool which has merely met its expectations? The way insurance company's do business now is not meant to be a true insurance process with integrity, it's something that insurance companies get away with because they can.

In summary, once you join a risk pool your rates should not go up.

Solution Part #2 - Shift Maintenance/Time Payment Plans to Doctors

Do we want maintenance costs to fall? Rather than have few dozen large insurance companies, why not have the patient deal directly with the doctor? Let's have patients set up "time payment" or "monthly membership" plans directly with an M.D. You will certainly get more and better competition from the 250,000 primary care doctors than from a few dozen large health insurance companies.

Think about this – 250,000 of the America's brightest minds all trying to figure out how to lower the costs of doing business so they can get more patients and provide better quality care. Think about how this "hive mind" would innovate when given the brand new challenge of increasing efficiency and lowering costs. Isn't this better than doctors sending bills to an insurance company and providing care without regard to price? Why would any doctor try to lower costs if the patient isn't even aware of the costs?

Will this be complex? Yes, at first. But doctors won't have to do it alone. In fact doctors can anticipate an enhanced industry of practice management and financial services to support this. No doctor will be left wanting for this kind of service. And of course prices for that will come down too, as well as the cost for handling insurance claims on anything and everything.

A more direct sell would unleash a flurry of economic activity as doctors self-organize, and support organizations grow. Doctors already have their "hive" mind organizations, but now will be sharing ways to be more cost effective.

And efficiency will improve radically. I once went into a dentist's office, with only a single dentist doing work. She had 3 employees in the reception area to handle reception, registration and records, and 2 insurance specialists to handle claims. From this I gather that the interface between doctors and insurance companies is a complex and expensive thing and less of it will be better.

Medical practices will communicate and companies selling solutions to help lower costs will spring up. A medical boom similar to the internet boom of the 1990's is not out of the question.

Would insurance companies hate this? They would make a stink certainly, but ultimately it doesn't hurt them that much. The key is to keep a level playing field so that no one is disadvantaged in the competition. Any business worth its salt will make money in a fair environment, as long as the rules are stable and the regulations they have to follow are clear and unambiguous. It is conceivable that insurance companies will come out well ahead by not having to process claims for lower dollar items.

Solution Part #3 - Businesses Should Not Buy Healthcare

Yes, I said it - your employer should not be providing health insurance. No, you're employer should be contributing to your tax free medical savings account so you can pay for your own! Here is a brief history and an outline our free enterprise logic for incentivizing lower health costs.

How World War II Created Employer-Sponsored Health Insurance

The history of employers providing workers with health insurance goes back several decades.

During World War II, when soldiers were being shipped off to war, domestic industry experienced a serious shortage of workers. Workers demanded wage increases but with a risk of wage hyperinflated salaries, federal government implemented wartime wage and price controls.

To grant a concession to labor without violating wage and price controls, Congress exempted employer-sponsored health insurance from wage controls and income taxation. The effect was to provide for increases in effective compensation for employees in the form of non-taxable health benefits. This created an enormous tax savings for the employee getting employer-sponsored health benefits, rather than purchasing health insurance with after-tax dollars. However, this did not stop after World War II. By the mid-1960s, employer-sponsored health benefits were almost universal.

So larger employers now find it necessary to provide health care to employees just to keep them. As a result, companies expend substantial management resources and risk the continued rise of health care costs as a total part of the compensation package.

The problem, again, is separation of the customer from the provider. I don't doubt that businesses care about their employees and want to provide the best possible benefits. But this is a case where businesses are ultimately buying a package designed for the business. The employee cannot shop based on price and quality, it's already done.

The solution - make it illegal for businesses to buy health insurance for their employees. I am not saying business should stop providing benefits. I am saying they should stop buying directly from insurance companies.

The answer is the expansion of something that already exists, the health savings account. Let's let the employer contribute to the employee's health savings plan. Let's also allow (i.e. require) the employee to pay for his own health insurance from this plan. This gives the employee a lot more flexibility in acquiring levels of benefits, yet keeps the benevolence of the employer intact. Ultimately this becomes more controllable and much less expensive for the employer as the management tail recedes and health costs become less expensive.

This is also much better for the employee. Now employees can shop for health plans that suit their needs. Once their plans accumulate enough to cover higher deductibles the employee can move to lower cost plans with a higher deductible.

The net result is employees making choices for health insurance on price and quality (perfect!). This increases competition and focuses the market on the needs of the employee rather than the needs of the employer.

Now let's increase the incentive. Let's loosen the regulations on the health savings plan so that money not spent servicing a health insurance or other health plan derivatives can be used to benefit the health of the employee in other ways. For example, why not allow things like vitamins, diet advice, health club memberships, perhaps even the occasional massage to be covered once the basic coverage is met? This could also pay for "health coaching" described later. With incentives on the table, employees suddenly will be much more responsible in managing their own health.

This could conceivably result in a healthier work force. Employees will spend more time thinking about their health and become more involved in the decision making regarding their health. Remember anything you subsidize you get more of. In this case we are subsidizing more responsible health management by the ultimate beneficiary, the individual.

Once the rules align properly and employees are properly incentivized to aggressively shop on price and quality, you'll find that businesses will naturally take this to the next level. Remember businesses are smarter than government.

Solution Part #4 – The Government's Role

The U.S. Government's role is substantial in our scenario, but not to manage people's lives and certainly not to provide its own insurance plan.

A. Templates

The first role of the government is to provide information. The average American is not equipped to judge an insurance plan nor can he grasp the intricacies involved in providing different levels of care. The medical terminology and treatment and pricing options for complex diseases and conditions are well beyond the grasp of the average Joe. However if we can find a way for the government to absorb the complexity and assume the risk of information misunderstanding, we can effectively reduce the complexity of a complex industry for the buyer.

Our solution in principle is simple. The government must research and provide "templates" for the various flavors of insurance plans, be it low cost, or high quality, or specialized to a particular medical condition. These are meant to be standard and complete plans but for information purposes only.

No insurance provider would be required to offer any of these templates as plans. However they would be required to compare their own plan to one of the templates and provide an "exception" document to potential customers. While a full blown insurance plan might be complicated and complex, the differences between full plan and a government certified "trusted" plan should have many fewer terms.

This gives consumers a much more stable starting point when they go shopping. They don't have to read entire policies and interpret the legal and medical intent. They can merely compare each to the familiar government template (which is stable, well scrutinized and can be studied in depth) and pick out the exceptions that matter. Then compare on price...

Tort reform, reducing medical lawsuits

In recent years I have heard much talk about tort reform in the medical malpractice lawsuits. The U.S. Government template system simplifies legal interpretation greatly.

It enables the government to have an information portal. If you search for your condition and the government portal says you are covered, then you are covered unless your plan's "exceptions" document says explicitly that it doesn't. This will save massively on lawsuits, since in any court case against an insurance company, only a much smaller and more explicit document must be considered.

Naturally these templates need to be airtight. But the major insurance companies are good at this. Bring in an IBM or an SAIC, partner with Google and this could be well done, probably for much less than the cost of the ObamaCare web portals ($5 Billion and counting at the time of this writing...)

B. *Work Breakdown Structures and X-prizes*

A second government role is also informational. The government (or perhaps a public/private partnership) should provide a "work breakdown structure" (WBS) for health care down to the most minute activity possible.

A work breakdown structure is a map of activities broken into its smallest manageable parts. For example, to treat the flu you might have the following breakdown - check in, assign a room, nursing attention, doctor attention, test to diagnose, prescribe a treatment, check out, send billing, and collect billing. Associate a cost with each of the activities and you will immediately see where and why any activity is expensive. A complete WBS will be massive, but well worth it.

The reason is very simple. If you break all of the possible activities down, then you have a chance to analyze and challenge each activity to see if it can be done less expensively, more effectively or faster. You may think this a daunting task, but insurance companies already produce "practice guides" with the bulk of the information needed.

Then let free enterprise, encouraged by government, insurance companies, doctors and philanthropists improve each step. Perhaps with an "X prize."

According to Xprize.org a purveyor of highly successful prizes for space, environmental issues, education and much more, "An XPRIZE is a highly leveraged, incentivized prize competition that pushes the limits of what's possible to change the world for the better. It captures the world's imagination and inspires others to reach for similar goals, spurring innovation and accelerating the rate of positive change."

X-prizes were used to encourage commercialization of space, and are incentivizing advances in robotics, cancer detection, Alzheimer's treatments, urban farming and much more. Put an X-prize on the expensive spots in the WBS and you will likely find a cheaper way to do it.

For example, some Doctors spend only 8 minutes, down from the 12 minutes optimum face to face (the common figure from a decade ago). It may seem like more, but of the hour and a half visit you see other folks and get shuffled from waiting room to examination room. A non-doctor runs a bunch of the tests, the doctor reads the results blowing two of your optimum 12 minutes. This is not a bad thing. An NIH study from 2005 says (3) that almost half of the day is spent outside of the examination room on patients not physically present (hello X prize folks!).

The USG can contribute to the X-prize, perhaps even working through private organizations. One can envision a marketplace or a crowdsourcing environment for tough and expensive parts of the WBS, where individuals, companies or the doctors themselves contribute $5 each for a solution they think may be important.

C. Doctors Rating System

A further government role could be to maintain data on price competition with doctors and insurance packages. People should know which is the least expensive and which are the highest quality. While ultimately private industry may provide a better solution, a rule setting effort from the government would provide useful and verifiable information to people shopping for healthcare.

It should be noted rating systems are always questionable and subject to gamesmanship. A number of competitive systems would be better than just one.

And let's remember to keep it limited and focused. The ObamaCare portal was a disaster; we do not want to repeat a $5 Billion dollar mistake.

Doctors have been conditioned to not have to advertise, and certainly not based on price and quality competition. They will have to figure out what quality aspects their patients desire from their practice and compete for new patients.

D. Encourage Cheaper Diagnosis and Treatments

If you look at the classic technology adoption models, perhaps Everett Roger's Innovation Adoption Lifecycle or Geoffrey Moore's model in

Crossing the Chasm, you find most technology is very expensive at first, to where only the well-off can afford it. That is also why NASA and military budgets are so high, because they must continually pay the highest prices to keep on the cutting edge. That's also why the most advanced medical equipment is in only the most exclusive hospitals at first.

Then early adopters get the equipment as the price goes down and then finally mass production makes technology affordable for a wide customer base and thus to the less affluent. This cycle has its roots not just in modern history but in ancient history as well. It's a natural cycle.

However, to some degree insurance prevents prices from dropping too far for a given procedure where cutting edge technology is involved. Prices drop to a certain extent but they have a natural "float" due to the interaction between doctors and insurance. Why would a doctor look for a cheaper service when it's paid for either way by insurance? He makes more money if the prices stay elevated and his patients don't have to pay for it.

With this price float at a higher level, the production calculations of equipment and drug manufacturers will be geared toward smaller quantities at a higher price point. But if a major part of diagnosis and maintenance are moved to the doctor's maintenance plan, competing on price and quality with hundreds of thousands of other doctors, the float goes away, cheaper becomes better, production goes up and prices come down.

Part of the Government's role must be to encourage the development of technologies that will make diagnosis and treatment cheaper for the end user without sacrificing performance.

As mentioned above, the work breakdown structure (WBS) is the first step. Identifying what constitutes "cheaper" and being able to quantify the savings (and the risks!) when a new procedure, drug or technique comes about is hugely important.

If a government agency or a private entity wants to encourage cost saving solutions to an expensive component, the WBS is a measurement tool to gauge progress. If a research institution wants to apply for a grant to make a component of the WBS cheaper, this is a good basis for evaluation. The return on investment and social good will be distinct and measurable.

Another product of the government could be a "standard" equipment suite for doctor's office. Like the insurance templates, doctors would acquire this equipment at their option. But regulations could be geared toward this and beneficial financing plans could be encouraged by the government (careful, after all this is a subsidy…). This would push production quantities of the equipment up massively with a corresponding decrease in price.

So if you can imagine the medical practice of the future, for a checkup you may only be in the doctor's office for five minutes, if at all. Perhaps the basic equipment is cheap enough to have at home, or perhaps you go to a booth at your local drugstore. All of the tests get taken and evaluated and if you have a physical complaint and actually need to see the doctor you talk to him via Skype (has to be some kind of high resolution video, this is already happening in some places).

Doctors would have the more sophisticated diagnosis equipment and the human repair kits for various ailments – flu, cuts, broken bones, diabetes, ED, etc. – which encompass 90% of why you go to the doctor. Right now an MRI scan costs on average $2600. This is because the machine itself costs is hugely expensive, plus the building, the required maintenance and special operators. However the lowest cost MRI's according to Medicare are only $474, so cheaper MRI's can be done. With some incentive (the right X-prize?), I think a $150 MRI could be routine. Perhaps the doctor's maintenance fee could cover even this level of diagnosis for his patients.

Again, the government would have no role in the management of services, but rather in the maintenance of the WBS and encouragement of developments through information and X prize strategies.

Effects on American Health Culture

Let's talk for a minute about how health care culture will likely change. Right now you go to a doctor's beautiful office, wait for an hour in a luxurious waiting room, see your doctor for 9 minutes, and then have your insurance pay vast sums. With travel and time for paperwork, it's a two hour or more experience.

There is a certain amount of ceremony to this, kind of like going to church, and partly designed to put doctors on a pedestal. This latter point is actually a good thing since often patients need that voice of authority to stick to a difficult medical regimen that might help them. In other words, you do what is good for you because the doctor is the wisest of all and knows what is best (and orders you to do it). It's a bit of beneficial demagoguery, traditional in health culture throughout history in America and around the world.

This works to a degree but is there a better way? In this age of common sense, if you can get a thorough checkup and accurate answers to your health concerns in five minutes instead of two hours, would you do it? It could be a bad thing for folks who respond only to the voice of authority and follow their prescriptions primarily out of respect for the doctor. But in America we are not that big on demagoguery anymore. And what if one does not have that discipline or doesn't quite understand the gravity of their treatment, or even is just not willing to be responsible for their own health? Can we help them meet their health goals other ways and teach them to be responsible rather than provide a blind support system for them?

If we work things right, health maintenance will become inexpensive, convenient and rich in information, context and options. Contact with a doctor will be rare, the exception rather than the routine. But how do we maintain or actually improve healthfulness in America? These are our predictions:

1. The rise of the "health coach"

The concept of a "health coach" could replace the doctor as a disciplinary figure, payable from the health savings account.

Advice and discipline in maintaining health and in monitoring treatment regimens will come from someone who is knowledgeable (perhaps nurses, or maybe even a new class of medically trained professional) but not a doctor. The "coach" position would be merely someone with whom you engage to meet your health goals, personal contact, interested in your well-being and urging you on. The health coach might also interface with (even be recommended by) your doctor and may help provide data to your doctor to keep him abreast of your progress. This more personal support will come with a substantial reduction in price but an increase in effectiveness.

Why an increase in effectiveness? The knowledge of a doctor is and should be authoritative, but maintaining health and/or implementing complex or difficult health regimens are a matter of motivation. Positive feedback and frequent contact from a compatible personality will be much more effective than a simple prescription from a doctor.

You will shop for your doctor based on knowledge and expertise, but you may shop for your health coach based on personality. Some people (including the author) need a certain amount of nagging, some may need an ogre, others may need more of a peer and a friend, still others may be motivated by youth and energy, or authority and wisdom. In many respects this is a "sales" position, since persuasion is the important aspect (since it is already backed up by a doctor's expertise...). Contact with another human being to reinforce health responsibility will, I believe, become the norm.

This solution has a lot of basis in human psychology. Social pressure in a coaching format would be a powerful influence. At this point, most Americans know what they should be doing to be healthier, but it's not always easy. In the absence of a "healthy pill," individual (as opposed to mass) social pressure is most likely to make headway into improving health in America.

A further observation, as family units and inter-generational contact become less pervasive (the trend since the 1970's), and portions of the population become more isolated, the health coach phenomena will provide more human contact to older people in a very beneficial way. It may also provide an excellent source of employment for younger people who can be trained quickly and whose youth and energy are in abundance. These youth might also benefit from contact with clients who are older, wiser and more experienced in the ways of the world.

A good health coach would need certain skills, perhaps in some cases to the level of a registered nurse, (but I think not always) with the ability to understand doctors prescriptions and prescribed regimens, with the ability to convey information to the doctor in the case of unexpected developments or uncooperative clients. With the rapid increase in medical technology, ahealth coach might even carry a suite of basic diagnostic tools, and be able to report vital signs and look for warning signs as specified by a doctor. These professionals would also come with expertise in shopping for healthcare plans and navigating federal programs.

A strict code of ethics would be required. These professionals would also need to be aware of HIPAA regulations with regard to keeping medical data private (perhaps the health coach would be given a log in to enter patient's data into the doctor's secure system).

2. People will have to be more responsible for their own health care.

ObamaCare and its attempt to provide everything for everyone (a failure by any measure) will be replaced with personal choice, and the ability to fail. The only way to improve health care is to have each individual take charge of his own and be motivated by self-interest. A "one-size-fits-all" approach from a socialized medical system can never compete with that.

3. Health care will be more convenient and comprehensive.

As described above, technology can make diagnosis widely available, cheap and convenient, if market conditions change to encourage it. What you do with it is your choice.

4. Health care will be within reach of everyone.

Yes, this means cheap and fast, perhaps most everything you need will be in a booth at your local drug store, where you insert $5 and spend 10 minutes. But you still have to take the step of getting it. Some people still won't. However with perhaps some encouragement from employers to take advantage of the advent of the health coach, a higher percentage of Americans will engage and be healthier.

5. The people who need the federal safety net will decrease substantially.

Prices will go down; people at lower economic levels will have less trouble paying for it. The federal safety net can fund health savings accounts for those who need it. But health care for those who need it can be funded through a version of the health savings plans, and these people will have to execute their own plan based on their choices.

6. Some people will still refuse to take responsibility, they will suffer for it.

It will be in the news when someone suffers or dies because they refuse to do what is good for them. It's happening now and will continue to happen. No method ever devised can force good habits and health on 100% of the 320 million people in America, nor should that be our goal. Accept it. Free will often means freedom to fail, let's work on getting people motivated, mourn the loss of people who could have helped themselves, but recognize this is both the blessing and a curse of a free nation.

Effects on Freedom of Religion

In the recent case of an organization run by Christians, Sylvia Burwell sued Hobby Lobby over its refusal to provide birth control in its health care plan.

This is an incredibly difficult and stupid problem with ObamaCare, and its half-assed implementation. ObamaCare imposes certain awkward requirements on health care provided by businesses owned by free Americans. In a free society business should have the right to compensate their employees how they choose and according to their own principles. Obama put the government in the worst possible situation, in conflict with culture, laws and the U.S. Constitution.

He has set himself up against the Pope, who leads a billion Catholics. How much of a conflict is this? A quote from John Paul VI:

"Responsible men can become more deeply convinced of the truth of the doctrine laid down by the Church on this issue if they reflect on the consequences of methods and plans for artificial birth control. Let them first consider how easily this course of action could open wide the way for marital infidelity and a general lowering of moral standards. Not much experience is needed to be fully aware of human weakness and to understand that human beings—and especially the young, who are so exposed to temptation—need incentives to keep the moral law, and it is an evil thing to make it easy for them to break that law. Another effect that gives cause for alarm is that a man who grows accustomed to the use of contraceptive methods may forget the reverence due to a woman, and, disregarding her physical and emotional equilibrium, reduce her to being a mere instrument for the satisfaction of his own desires, no longer considering her as his partner whom he should surround with care and affection."

Does it sound like there is any wiggle room here?

The Opposite of ObamaCare strategy restores the freedom of employers to provide the benefits they intend for their employees, while allowing the employees to buy health service a la carte based on their needs, and of course, quality and price. If you don't need birth control, you do not have to add it as part of your plan. Your employer has nothing to do with it.

This alleviates a recent question as to whether a company's insurance plan must pay for birth control or other services objectionable to certain religions. If the company merely pays into a health savings account and the employer buys their own plan, the problem is solved. Get the government out of the loop; return the choices to the individual.

Effects on the Economy

Let's run some numbers...

Health care is currently about 17% of our Gross National Product or about $2.9 Trillion annually. Let's make some very rough educated guesses and say this is a productive center with a nominal profit of 10%. I don't know of any studies covering this estimate so I will use the numbers I can conveniently manipulate. So let's say that $290 Billion is the annual free enterprise (or "positive feedback") benefit from the health care industry.

ObamaCare attempts to socialize this massive part of our GDP. I know the general effects of socialism changing from a positive result to a "negative feedback" system, and want to estimate the magnitude. Let's say this impact changes the health care industry from a 10% plus to a 10% minus. That's a $580 Billion swing on our $17 Trillion economy, or about a 3.4% permanent loss to our GNP growth. This might be offset somewhat by the black market effects that will certainly appear, but more likely the black market services for well-off Americans will largely manifest in foreign countries.

Just to put this in perspective, a 4% GDP growth is a booming economy, 3% is a great economy, 2% is a dragging economy, and 1% is trouble, lower than 0% is a recession. If a recession happens for more than 2 quarters it's a depression. We have had recession/depression conditions recently, it is not fun.

The other point is even though health care will be $580 Billion short in its productivity, at $2.32 Trillion, it will still cost $2.61 Trillion (the total minus the 10% profit). That means the government will have to make up the $290 Billion shortfall. That's an extra $900 per year per person in taxes (or added to the national debt) when spread over 320 million people. That is the result of "negative feedback," the government has to increase taxes to support a formerly self-supporting industry.

The numbers I've used are very approximate but the qualitative result is correct. If ObamaCare is not repealed and replaced with something with a free enterprise philosophy, the socialist aspect of ObamaCare will take its toll in making health care less productive. To lose 3.4% in the current economy (2014 GDP was estimated at 2.4%), would take us from a dragging economy to a long lasting depression.

Medical Technology and Progress in the Near Term

The Technology Advances

From a technology standpoint we live in exciting times! As I mentioned, I'm no expert on healthcare, but I am a diehard technologist. Some amazing and promising medical techniques under development could substantially affect the high price of medical care. The key, as mentioned before, is to change the industry to allow self-interested competition, based on a price and quality, to naturally encourage less expensive medical procedures.

Much is already underway. For example Elizabeth Holmes founded a company called Theranos. She and her company have developed a process to radically increase the speed and reduce the costs of many standardized blood tests. This by itself could substantially reduce diagnostic costs. She's a billionaire and rightfully so. In my opinion she's an American hero.

Will she put some labs out of business? Quite possibly. But free enterprise is all about creative destructiveness, new solutions supplant the old, and we move on.

New cancer treatments are emerging quickly, with new materials, genetics, nano-materials and viral vectors. These amazing technologies and innovations will be the future of medical care. And depending on how we encourage their development, they could be boutique technologies for the wealthy, or inexpensive equipment for every doctor's office.

The new technologies are truly incredible.

3-D printing of Human Organs – 3D printers build three dimensional models of objects out of a variety of special materials. It turns out by using certain kinds of human cells as the building material they can actually construct human replacement parts. Much of the 3D printer technology developed for the medical field is adapted from commercially available 3D printers, so this doesn't have to be expensive.

3-D printing seems like a novelty (Yes! You can make a doll with your face!) but the medical world is 3D printing multi-layered skin, ears, bones, parts of kidneys, blood vessels, vascular grafts, tracheal splints, heart tissue and cartilaginous structures (4). More sophisticated structures on can be grown on "scaffolds" to support the organ while it grows.

3-D printing also has the potential to build prosthetics and other items at radically reduced costs, including moving limbs. With the application of age old drafting and design software, items can be customized to fit a human being, delivering them quickly and efficiently to the patient. (5)(6)(7)

Robotic surgery (8) is catching on as well, remote diagnosis and so much more.

Re-growing human body parts - Researchers have also been able to grow a beating human heart, and have been able to regrow complete body parts for lab rats. (9)(10) This technology shows a great deal of promise for replacing even the most complex human organs.

Diagnosis quickly and effectively – A simple scan of the tech world finds technologies for diagnosing diseases and ailments quickly and effectively. The seemingly magic Star Trek medical "tri-corder" for taking vital statistics and diagnosing diseases could be realized in short order. In fact there is a $10 million X prize for it. Prototype testing and evaluation is underway right now. (11)(12)

How about something that sniffs your feet for diabetes related infections? A machine known as the Cyranose320 can do it in less than a minute. How about a test on a single drop of blood to quickly ascertain every virus you have ever encountered? The VirScan method is doing it, and inexpensively. How about a method for using a laser to analyze your breath to sniff out infections and possibly cancer? University of Adelaide in Australia is working on it. Researchers from Florida Atlantic University have created a sensitive film that can detect viruses and bacteria, such as HIV and Staph, at home. It plugs right into your smart phone for interpretation, and you can send the results right to you doctor. Manu

Prakesh at Standford University has invented a hand crank device to run 15 tests. In mass production this will cost in the $5 range. (13)(14)(15)(16)

These relatively inexpensive diagnostic tools are hitting the medical field right now. Can you imagine designing a comprehensive suite of these tools doing a complete diagnosis on an ailing patient in a very short time? And of course without the massive hospital costs, at least for the first round.

You can already see a doctor without leaving your home. Doctors on Demand can diagnose and treat a number of common ailments through a "video visit," such as the common cold, sore throat, UTIs, sports injuries, skin rashes, eye conditions and more. At this stage, of course, more complex conditions still require a doctor's visit. (17)

The Evolution?

Without the pressure of free enterprise we will still see all of these benefits come to fruition, but the prices will be premium and unaffordable. On the other hand if you can arrange for 970,000 doctors to compete for patients, you will see development of these great technologies lean toward lower costs as patients shop for doctors based on price and quality.

With the "Opposite" strategy, I predict the cost of diagnosis will fall dramatically as new technology comes online with price in mind. Companies that develop medical technology necessarily have large budgets to develop products. They have two directions they can go. They can add bells and whistles to make the equipment faster and easier to use, or they take the same functionality and make it less expensive.

Believe or not it's not the doctors or the technology people who make these decisions. The manufacturer's marketing and accounting folks will spend hundreds of thousands of dollars to look at the demand, survey the potential customers, do testing to see how the equipment sells at various price points. Ultimately they will come up with one demand curve based on price and another that plots price point versus profit. The price point is determined by the maximum estimated profit. Businesses are good at this and accurate in their estimates.

In free enterprise, this is a good thing because those curves will reflect the needs and desires of the customers they are meant to serve, in this case the doctors. In a newly competitive free enterprise system, the doctors may demand less expensive equipment that will handle 95% of their needs rather than equipment 10 times more expensive that handles 98% (figures for illustration only...). Equipment manufacturers will channel their development accordingly producing a higher volume at a lower price. Higher volumes of equipment means more availability, resulting higher health care quality.

The Effects of Crowdsourcing

In this (my own) field, I have some expertise, not in health care but in something called "crowdsourcing." Crowdsourcing is where massive number of people (for example 970,000 doctors, massive additional number of non-healthcare experts, and millions the general public) could look through this highly detailed work breakdown structure (WBS, as mentioned previously) and generate ideas on how to increase efficiency.

Crowdsourcing could be integrated with the WBS. If someone posts an idea that might work, each individual doctor may decide if the idea meets the criteria for his personal X prize. The better the idea, the more prize money received. In this manner we are "crowdsourcing" both the idea side and the incentive side. It's a natural result, in fact exactly why the work breakdown structure was invented in the first place.

Conclusion

Free enterprise approaches are powerful and effective. Informed individual choice is the best way to provide health care, and is the only ideal compatible with American principles of freedom. But with choice comes responsibility.

Socialist approaches like ObamaCare are weak and ineffective. In fact it has been a major shift away from American philosophies of freedom, free enterprise and personal responsibility. If we move rapidly we can certainly prevent ObamaCare from further destroying a major part of our economy and sending health care pricing to the point of unaffordability.

If this makes you as angry as it does me, contact your Congressman and let him know. If you see him at an event, ask him why Obamacare is still in force. And feel free to recommend this book "The Opposite of ObamaCare."

References

(1) Flashboys, http://michaellewiswrites.com

(2) Health Insurance Profit Ratios,
http://csimarket.com/Industry/industry_Profitability_Ratios.php?s=800

(3) Time spent with Patients,
http://www.ncbi.nlm.nih.gov/pmc/articles/PMC1466945/

(4) Tony Stark Gives Boy A Bionic Arm, http://www.popsci.com/tony-stark-gives-boy-bionic-arm-video

(5) Extreme bionics, http://www.popsci.com/sxsw-2015-how-extreme-bionics-will-help-rid-world-disability

(6) Retinal Prosthesis, http://www.2-sight.com/g-the-argus-ii-prosthesis-system-pf-en.html

(7) Body parts can be 3-d printed,
http://www.popsci.com/science/gallery/2013-07/5-body-parts-scientists-can-3-d-print

(8) Robotic surgery, http://www.buzzfeed.com/abagg/watch-a-tiny-robot-perform-surgery-on-a-wounded-grape

(9) A tiny beating human heart, http://www.popsci.com/researchers-grow-first-ever-beating-hearts-stem-cells

(10) A lab grown rat arm, http://www.popsci.com/wave-hello-first-lab-grown-rat-arm-video

(11) Star Trek style Tricorder, http://spectrum.ieee.org/tech-talk/biomedical/devices/first-prototype-of-a-working-tricorder-unveiled-at-sxsw

(12) Bio-sensing films help diagnose diseases remotely, http://www.popsci.com/new-smartphone-platform-can-detect-infectious-diseases-anywhere

(13) Test lab in a music box, http://www.popsci.com/medical-lab-music-box

(14) Blood scan reveals every virus http://www.popsci.com/virscan-detects-patients-history-viral-infections-drop-blood

(15) Sniffing feet for infections, http://www.popsci.com/sniffing-feet-infection

(16) Laser breathalyzer sniffs out disease, http://www.popsci.com/laser-breathalyzer-can-sniff-out-disease

(17) Doctors can provide checkups remotely, http://www.doctorondemand.com/

Made in the USA
Lexington, KY
11 April 2018